This book belongs to:

_____

- -

_____

_____

- -

_____

Name: _____

DIRECTIONS: TRACE AND PRACTICE WRITTING THE LETTER BELOW

1. Read

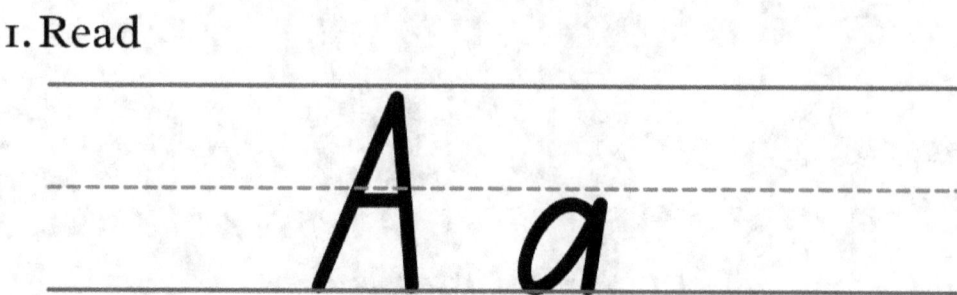

2. Trace

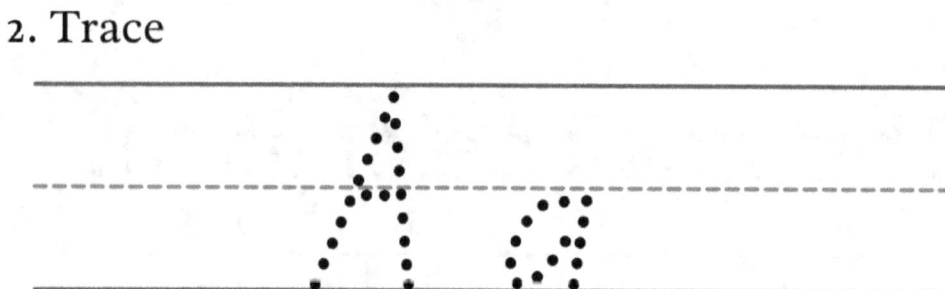

3. Practice

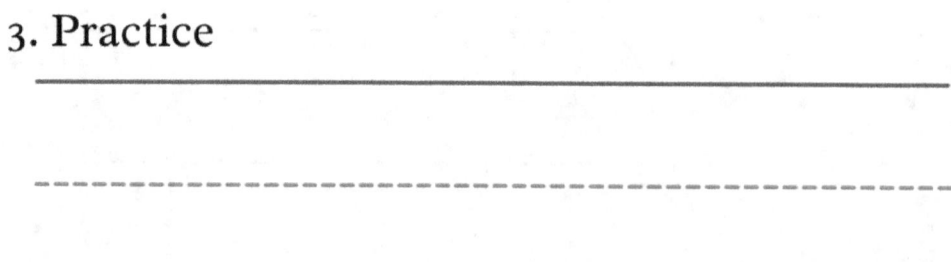

Name: _____

DIRECTIONS: TRACE AND PRACTICE WRITTING THE LETTER BELOW

1. Read

2. Trace

3. Practice

Name: _____

DIRECTIONS: TRACE AND PRACTICE WRITTING THE LETTER BELOW

1. Read

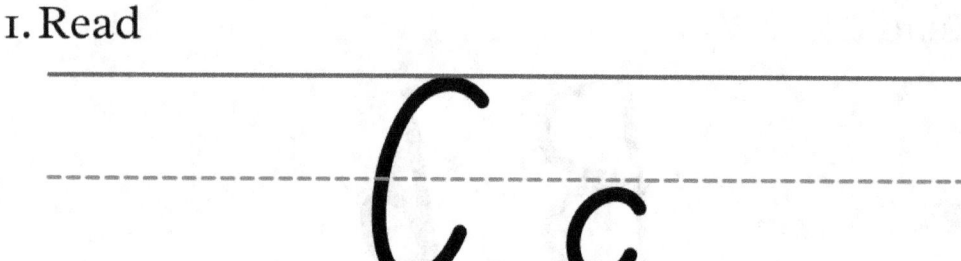

2. Trace

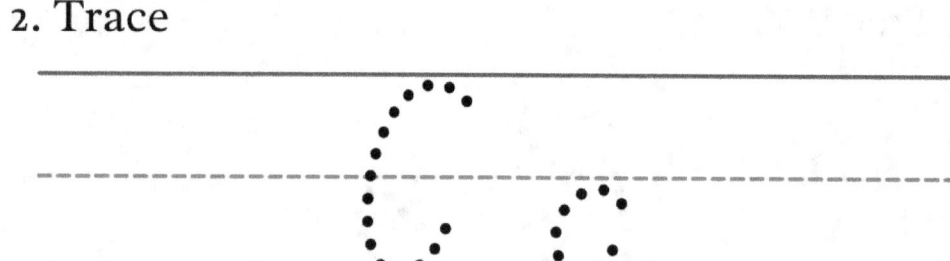

3. Practice

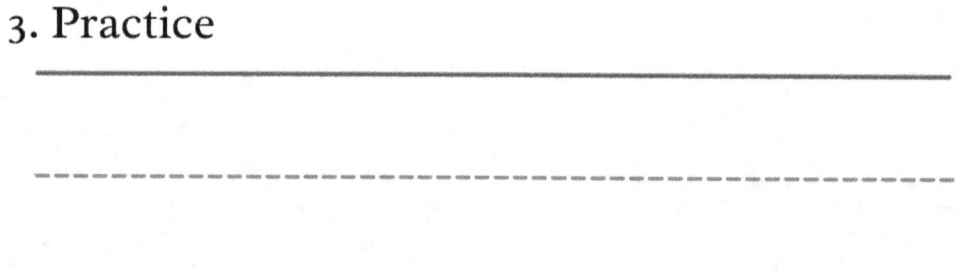

Name: _____

DIRECTIONS: TRACE AND PRACTICE WRITTING THE LETTER BELOW

1. Read

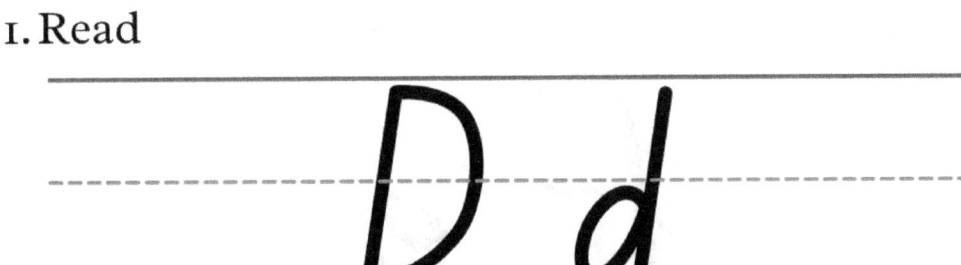

2. Trace

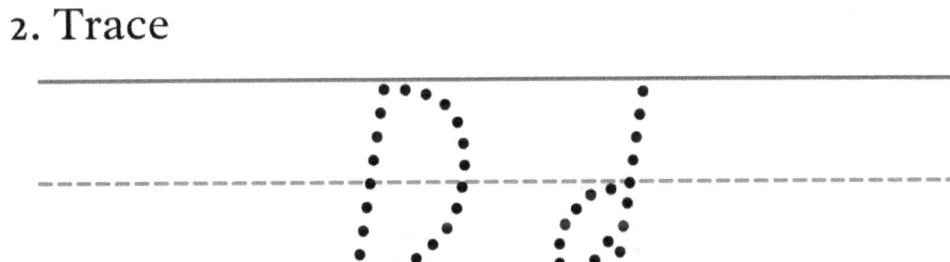

3. Practice

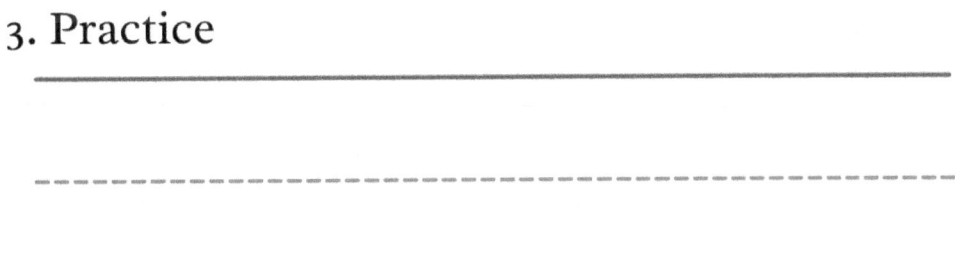

Name: _____

DIRECTIONS: TRACE AND PRACTICE WRITTING THE LETTER BELOW

1. Read

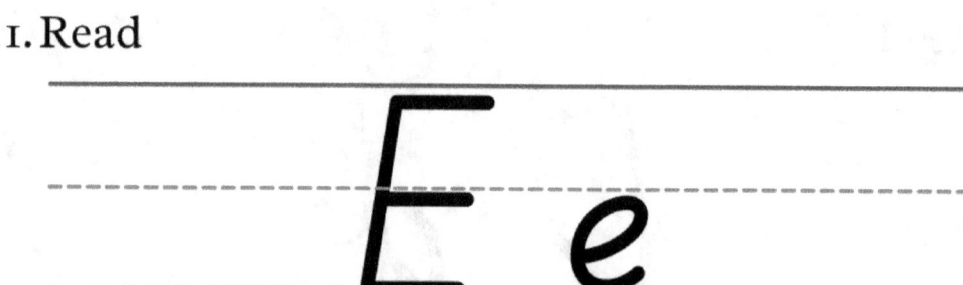

2. Trace

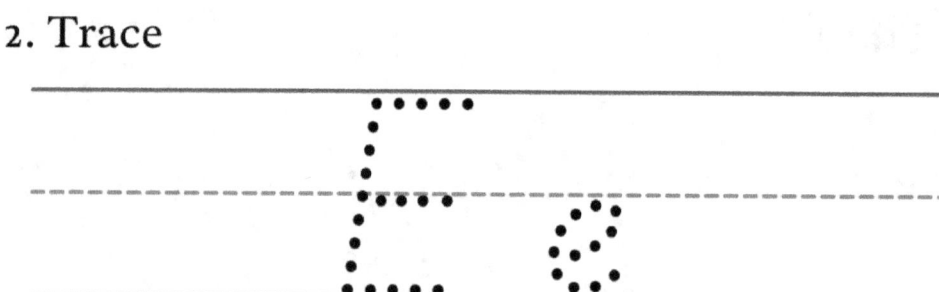

3. Practice

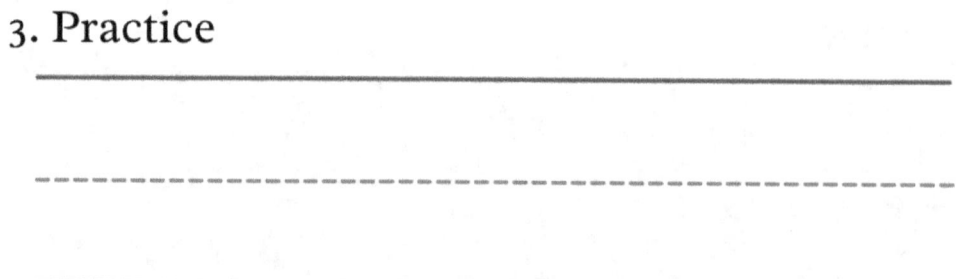

Name:

DIRECTIONS: TRACE AND PRACTICE WRITTING THE LETTER BELOW

1. Read

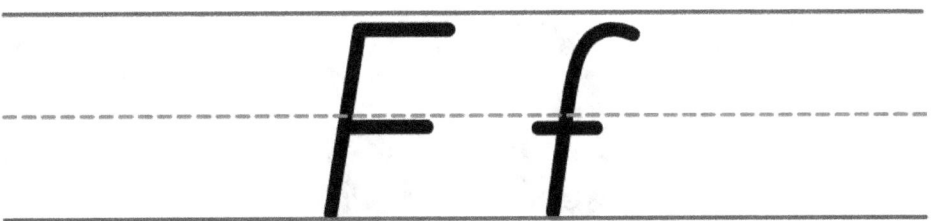

2. Trace

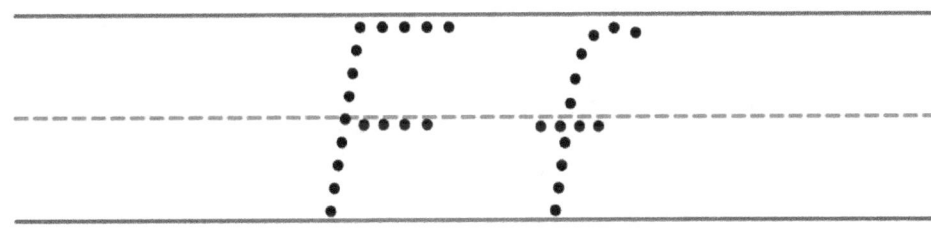

3. Practice

Name:

DIRECTIONS: TRACE AND PRACTICE WRITTING THE LETTER BELOW

1. Read

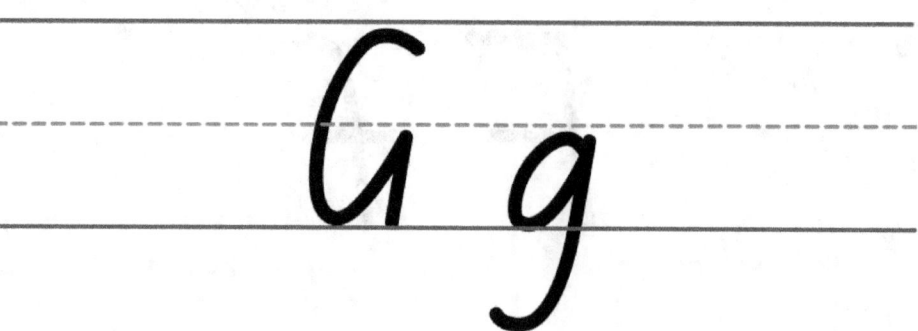

2. Trace

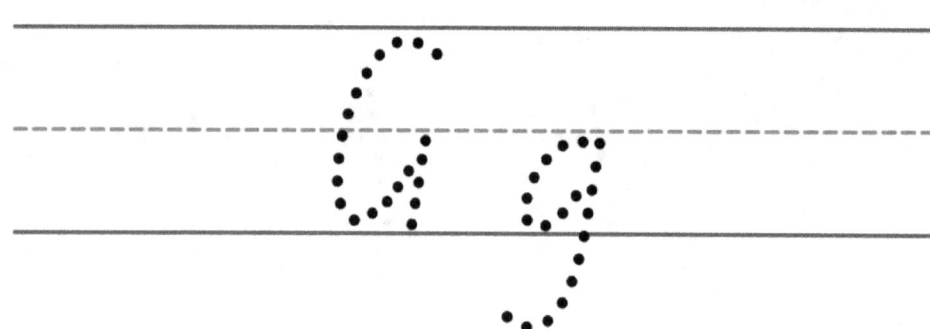

3. Practice

Name:

DIRECTIONS: TRACE AND PRACTICE WRITTING THE LETTER BELOW

1. Read

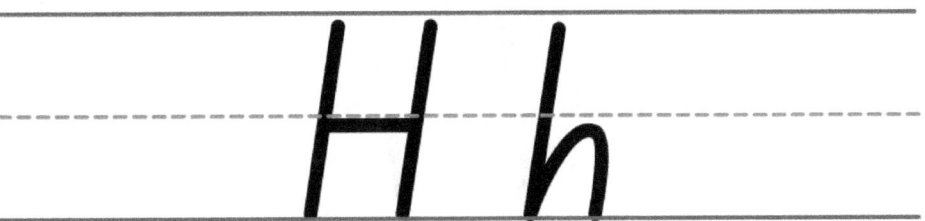

2. Trace

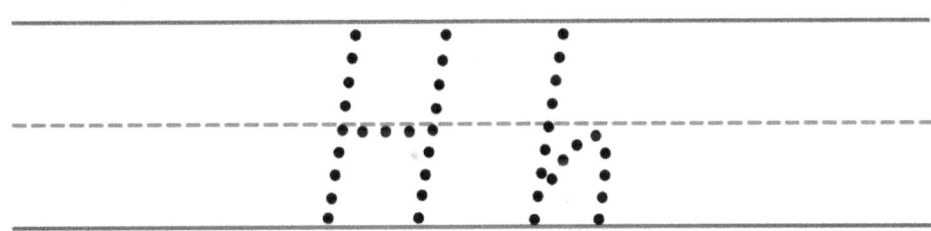

3. Practice

Name: _____

DIRECTIONS: TRACE AND PRACTICE WRITTING THE LETTER BELOW

1. Read

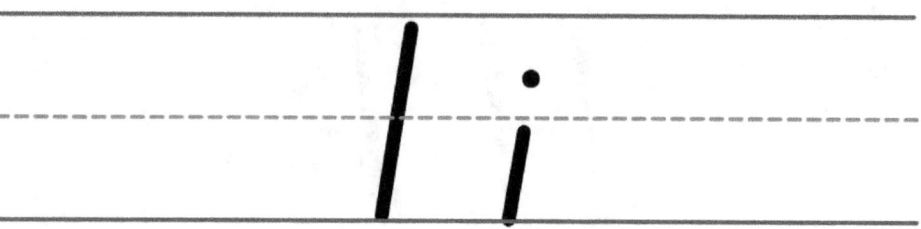

2. Trace

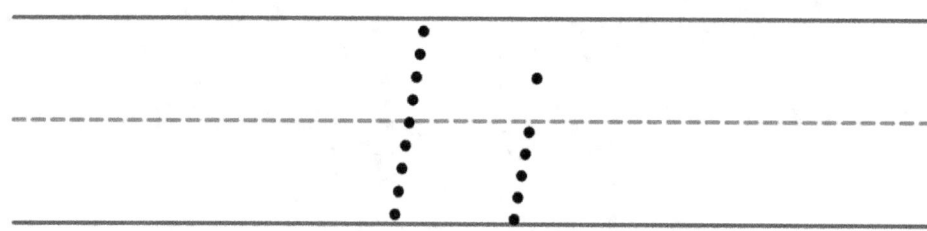

3. Practice

Name:

DIRECTIONS: TRACE AND PRACTICE WRITTING THE LETTER BELOW

1. Read

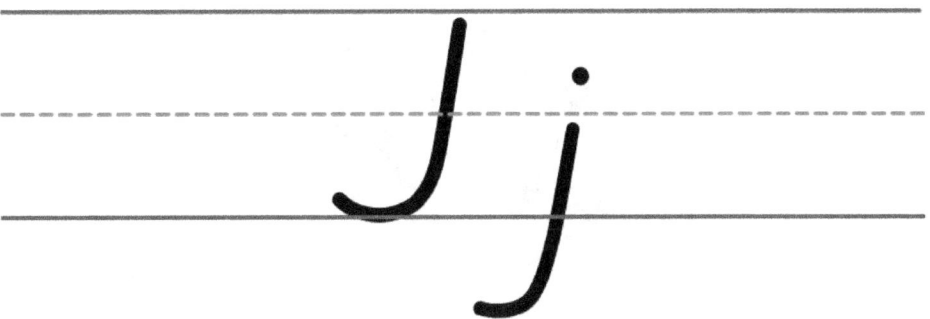

2. Trace

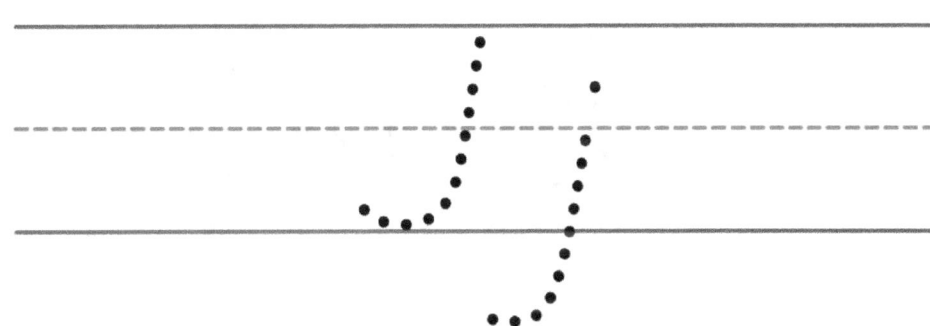

3. Practice

Name: _____

DIRECTIONS: TRACE AND PRACTICE WRITTING THE LETTER BELOW

1. Read

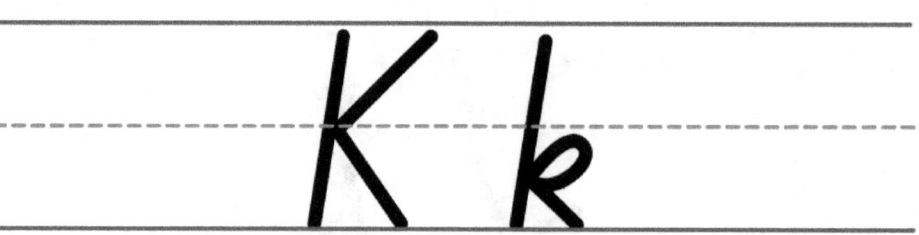

2. Trace

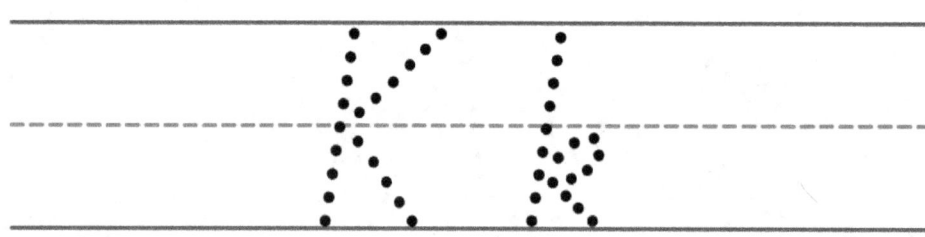

3. Practice

Name: _____

DIRECTIONS: TRACE AND PRACTICE WRITTING THE LETTER BELOW

1. Read

2. Trace

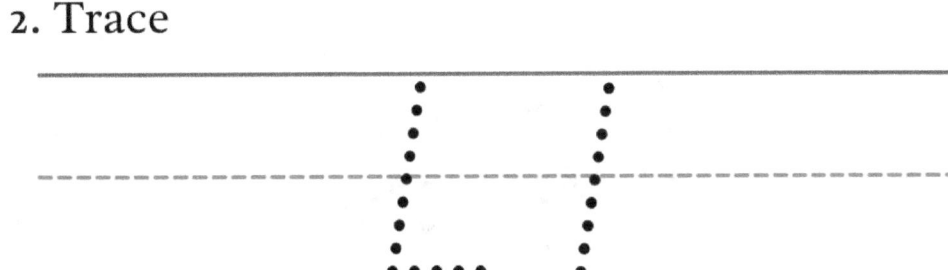

3. Practice

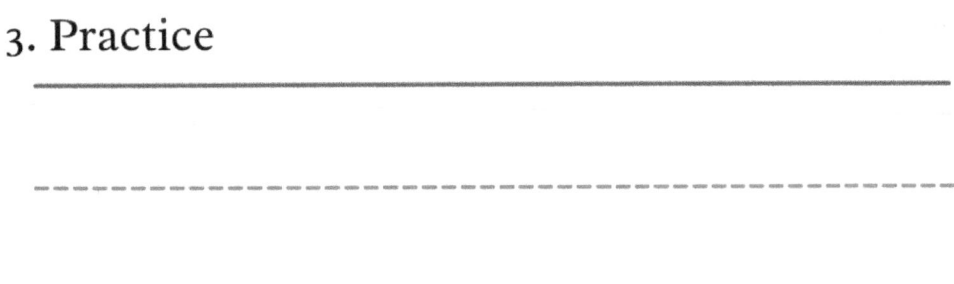

Name:

DIRECTIONS: TRACE AND PRACTICE WRITTING THE LETTER BELOW

1. Read

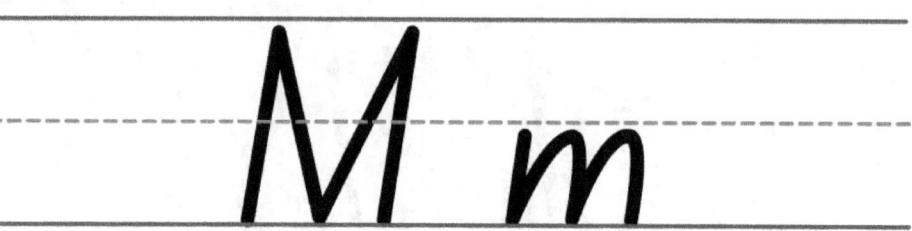

2. Trace

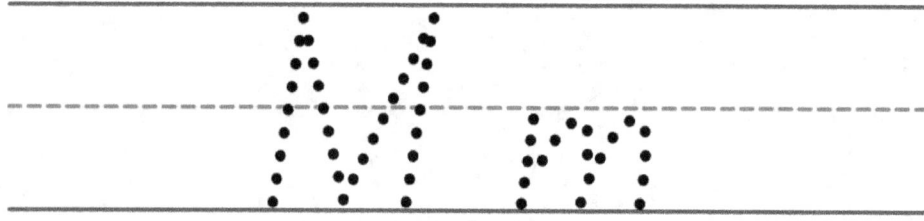

3. Practice

Name: _____

DIRECTIONS: TRACE AND PRACTICE WRITTING THE LETTER BELOW

1. Read

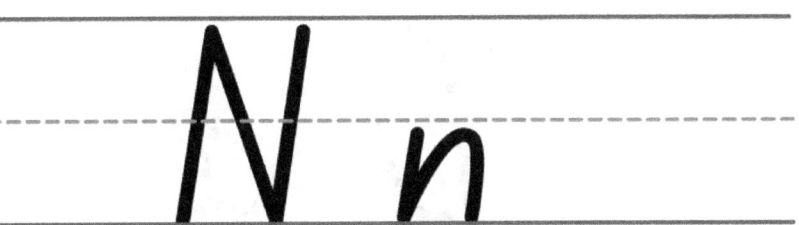

2. Trace

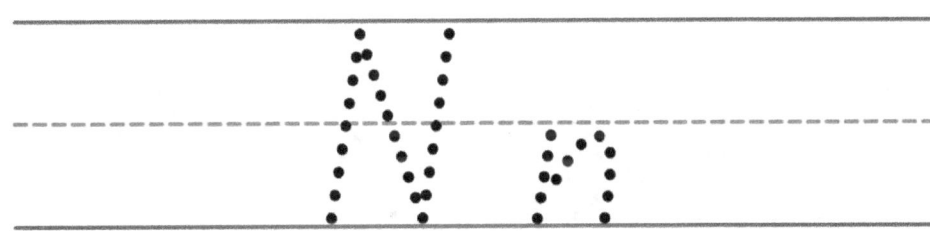

3. Practice

Name: _____

DIRECTIONS: TRACE AND PRACTICE WRITTING THE LETTER BELOW

1. Read

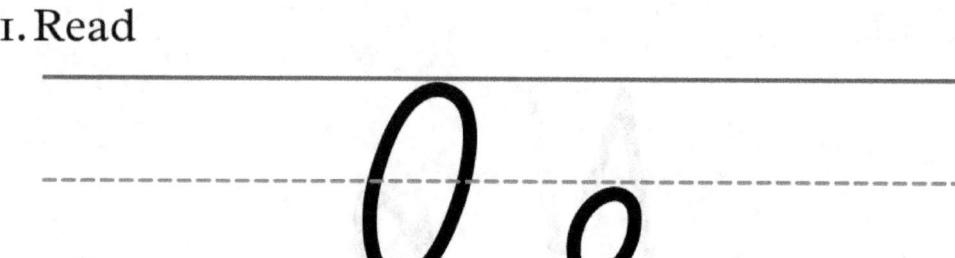

2. Trace

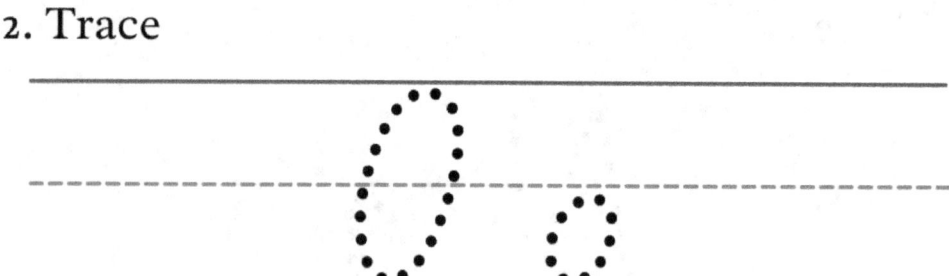

3. Practice

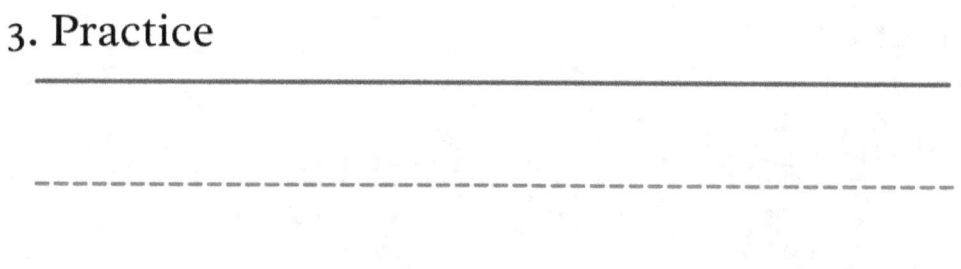

Name:

DIRECTIONS: TRACE AND PRACTICE WRITTING THE LETTER BELOW

1. Read

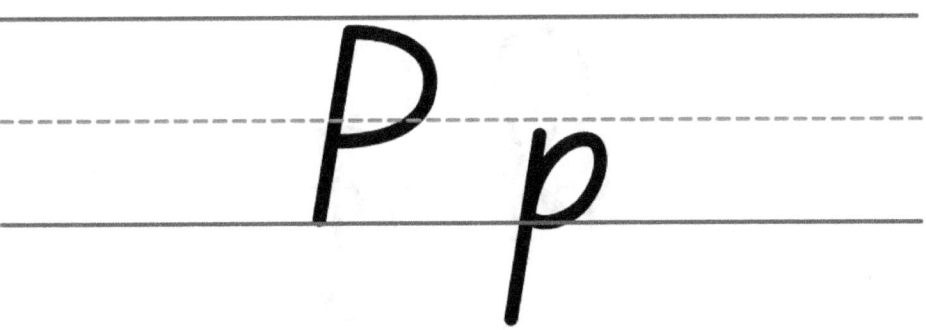

2. Trace

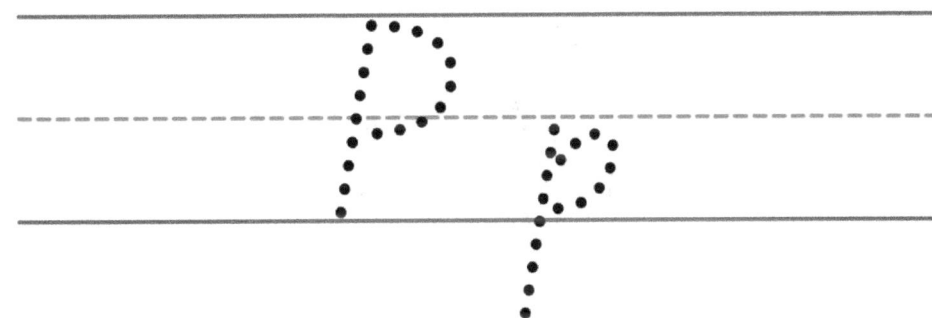

3. Practice

Name: _____

DIRECTIONS: TRACE AND PRACTICE WRITTING THE LETTER BELOW

1. Read

2. Trace

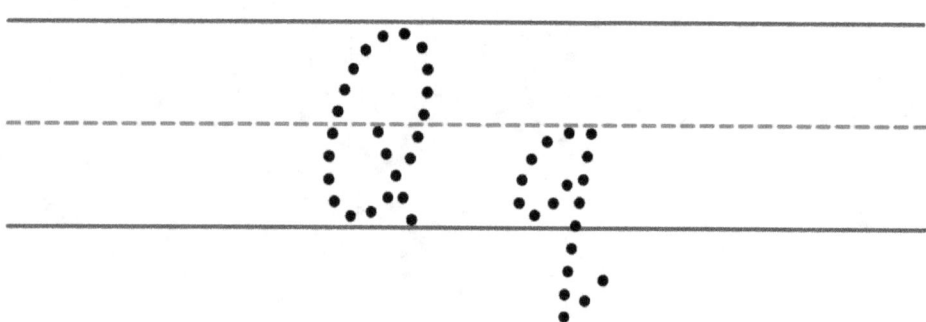

3. Practice

Name: _____

DIRECTIONS: TRACE AND PRACTICE WRITTING THE LETTER BELOW

1. Read

2. Trace

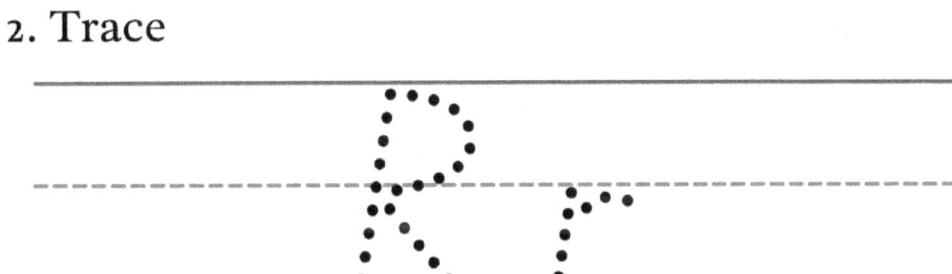

3. Practice

Name: _____

DIRECTIONS: TRACE AND PRACTICE WRITTING THE LETTER BELOW

1. Read

2. Trace

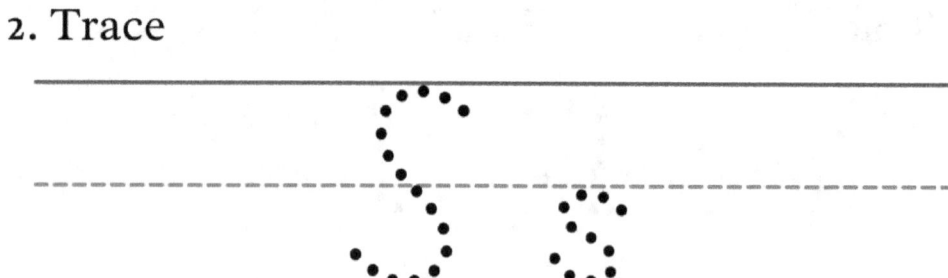

3. Practice

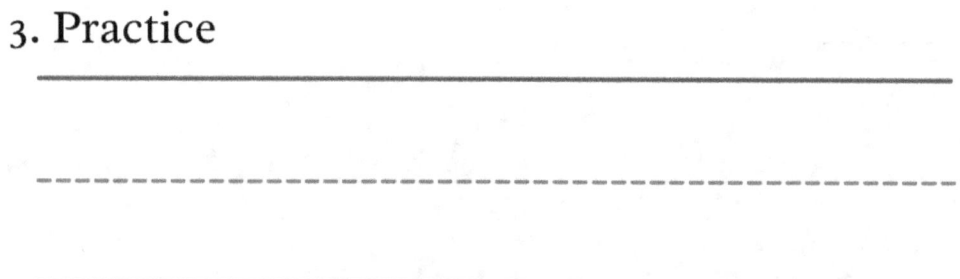

Name:

DIRECTIONS: TRACE AND PRACTICE WRITTING THE LETTER BELOW

1. Read

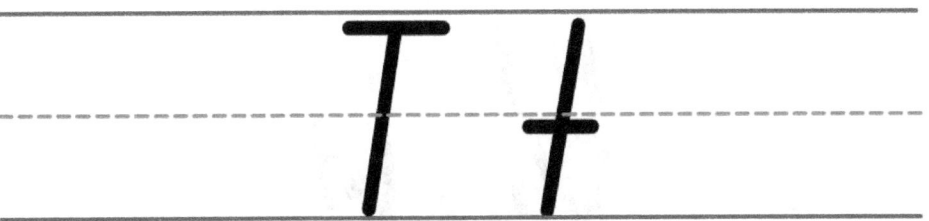

2. Trace

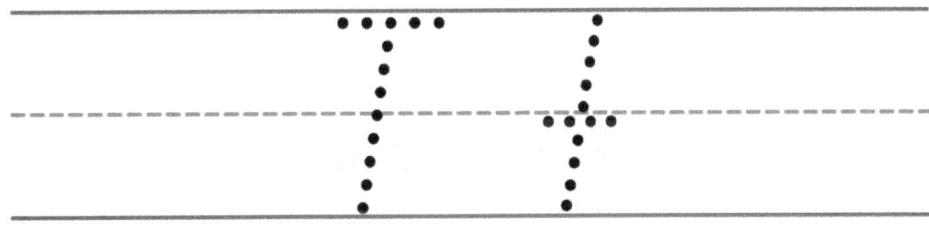

3. Practice

Name:

DIRECTIONS: TRACE AND PRACTICE WRITTING THE LETTER BELOW

1. Read

2. Trace

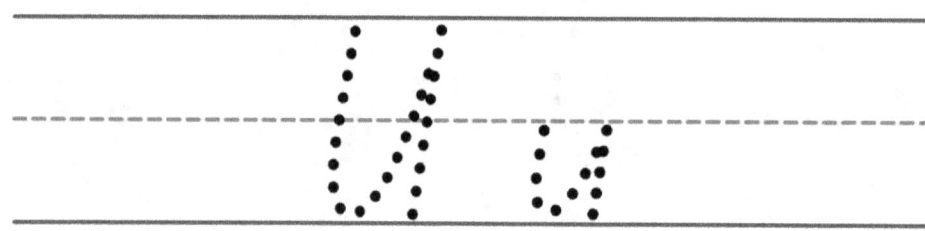

3. Practice

Name: _____

DIRECTIONS: TRACE AND PRACTICE WRITTING THE LETTER BELOW

1. Read

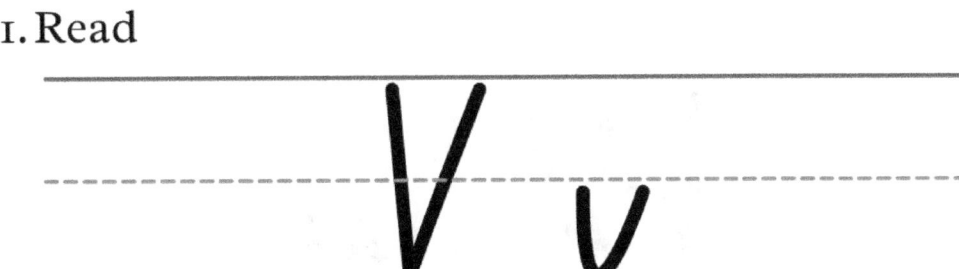

2. Trace

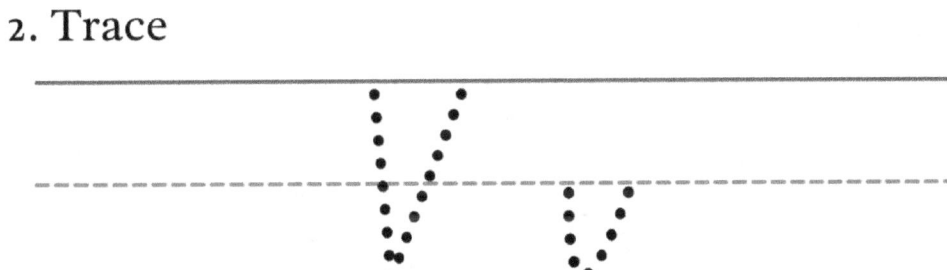

3. Practice

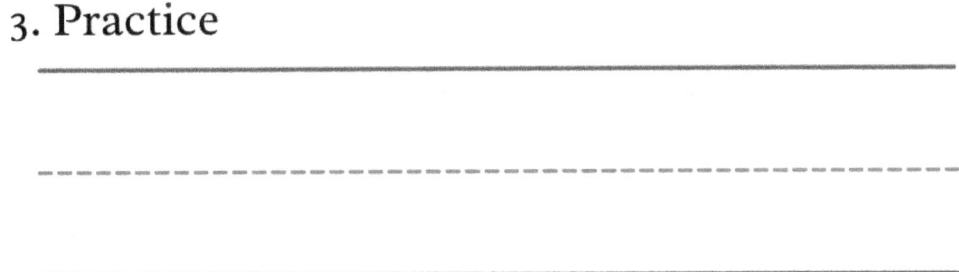

Name:

DIRECTIONS: TRACE AND PRACTICE WRITTING THE LETTER BELOW

1. Read

2. Trace

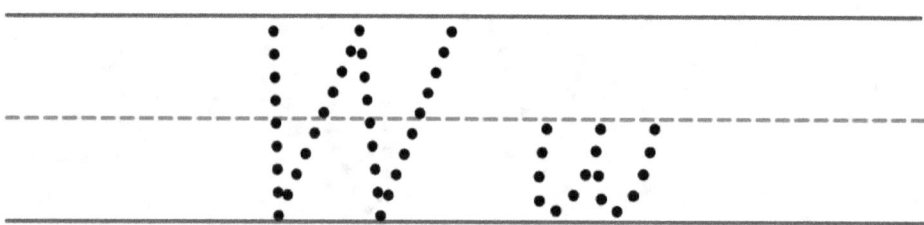

3. Practice

Name: _____

DIRECTIONS: TRACE AND PRACTICE WRITTING THE LETTER BELOW

1. Read

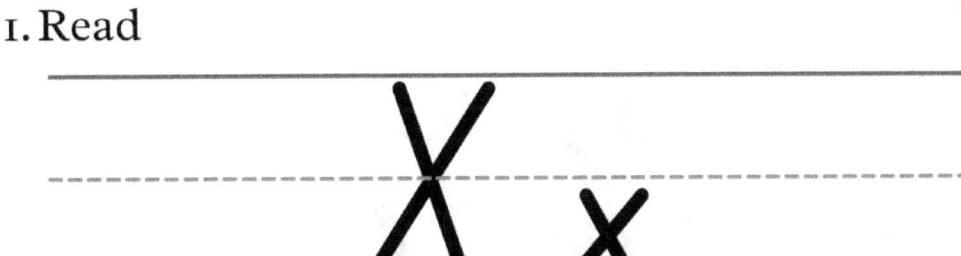

2. Trace

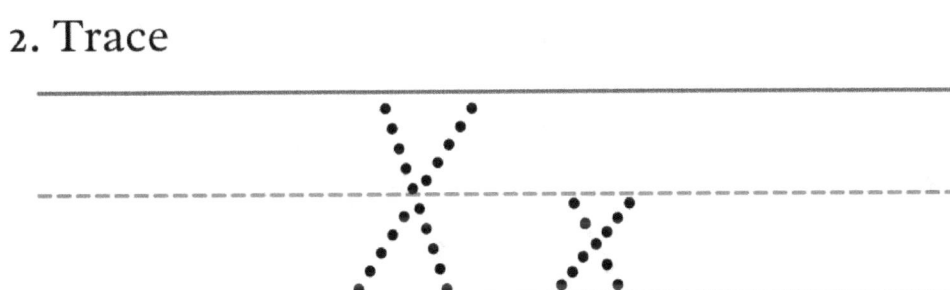

3. Practice

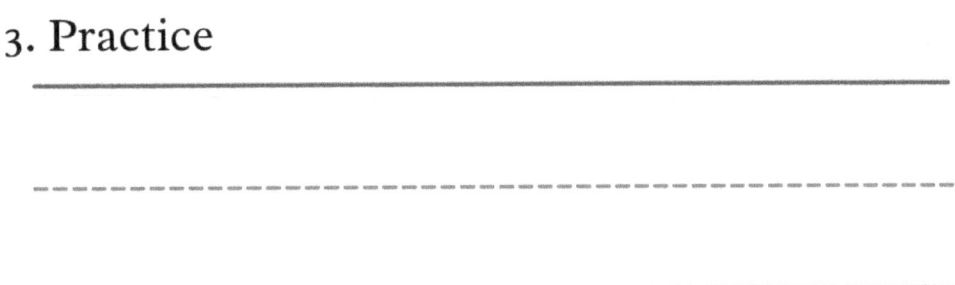

Name:

DIRECTIONS: TRACE AND PRACTICE WRITTING THE LETTER BELOW

1. Read

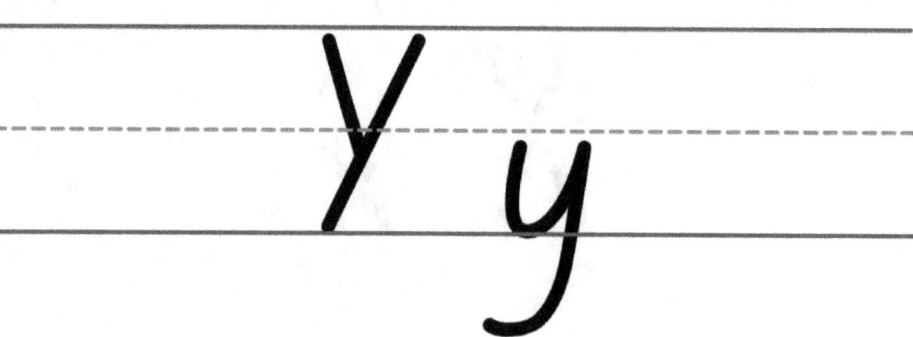

2. Trace

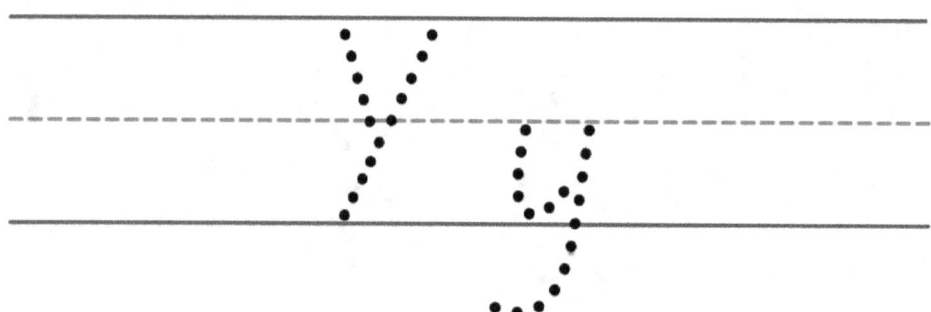

3. Practice

Name: _____

DIRECTIONS: TRACE AND PRACTICE WRITTING THE LETTER BELOW

1. Read

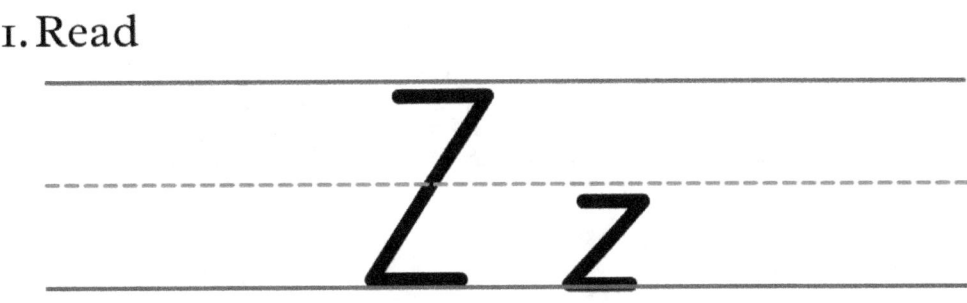

2. Trace

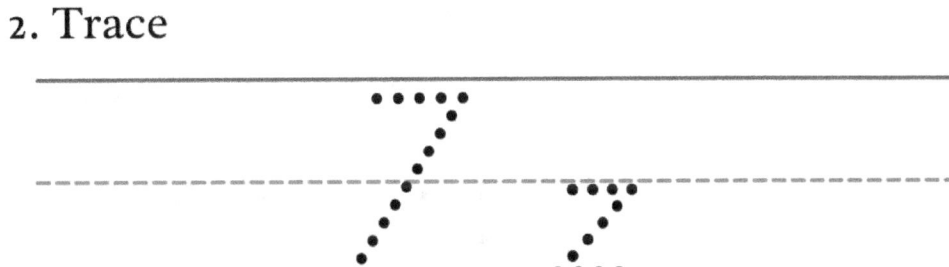

3. Practice

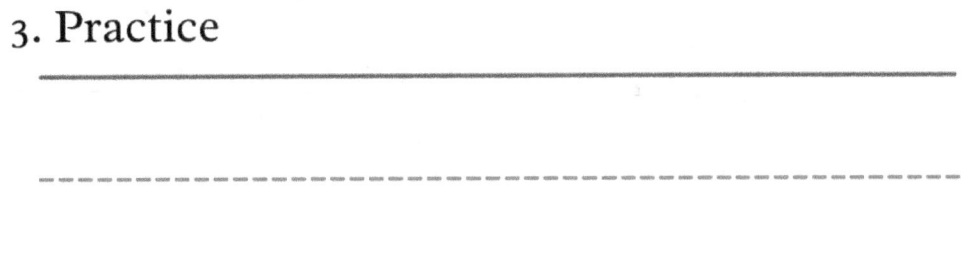

Name: _____

DIRECTIONS: TRACE THE WORDS THAT BEGIN WITH THE LETTER A

Name: _____

DIRECTIONS: WRITE THE WORDS THAT BEGIN WITH THE LETTER A

Name: _____

DIRECTIONS: TRACE THE WORDS THAT BEGIN WITH THE LETTER B

Name: _____

DIRECTIONS: WRITE THE WORDS THAT BEGIN WITH THE LETTER B

Name: _____

DIRECTIONS: TRACE THE WORDS THAT BEGIN WITH THE LETTER C

Name: _____

DIRECTIONS: WRITE THE WORDS THAT BEGIN WITH THE LETTER C

Name: _____

DIRECTIONS: TRACE THE WORDS THAT BEGIN WITH THE LETTER D

Name: _____

DIRECTIONS: WRITE THE WORDS THAT BEGIN WITH THE LETTER D

Name: ______________________________

DIRECTIONS: TRACE THE WORDS THAT BEGIN WITH THE LETTER E

ear

egg

earth

eggplant

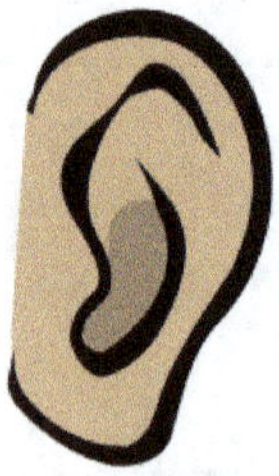

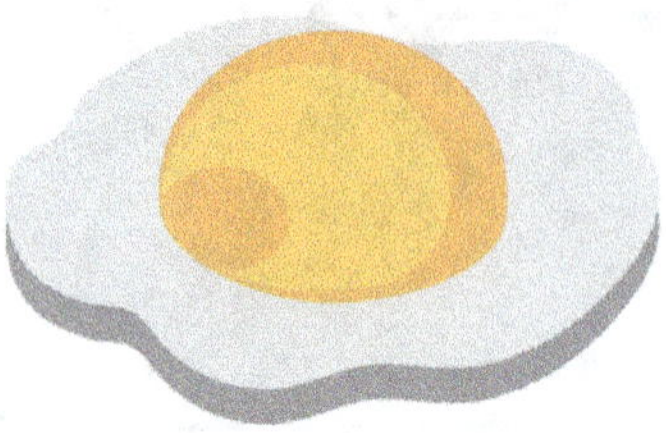

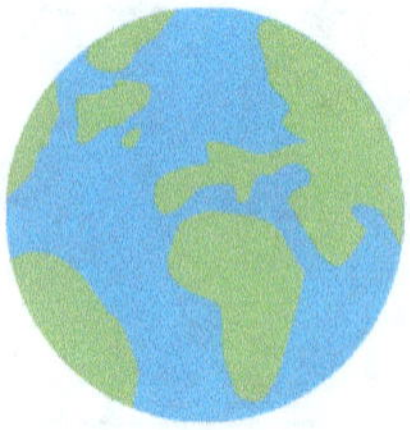

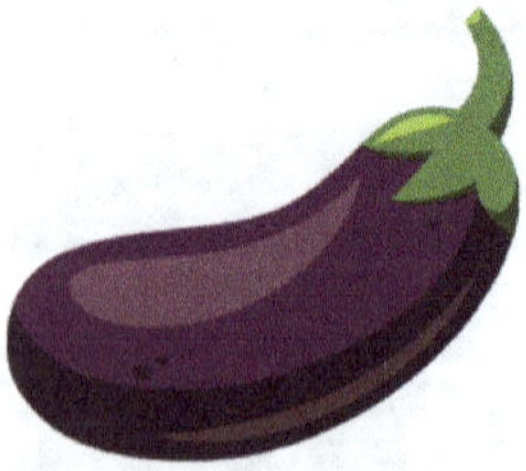

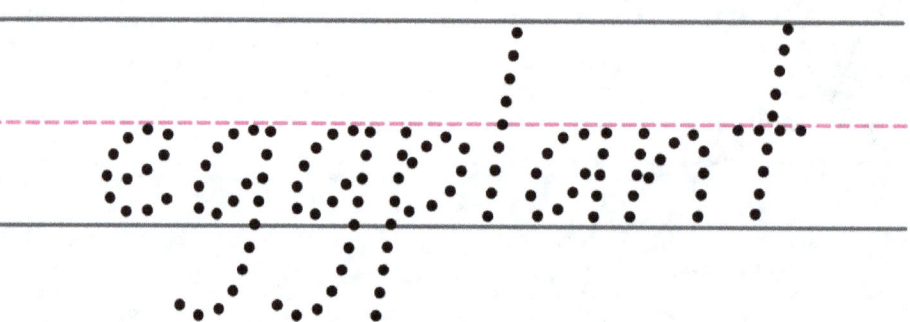

Name: _____

DIRECTIONS: WRITE THE WORDS THAT BEGIN WITH THE LETTER E

Name: _____

DIRECTIONS: TRACE THE WORDS THAT BEGIN WITH THE LETTER F

Name: _____

DIRECTIONS: WRITE THE WORDS THAT BEGIN WITH THE LETTER F

Name: _____

DIRECTIONS: TRACE THE WORDS THAT BEGIN WITH THE LETTER G

Name: _____

DIRECTIONS: WRITE THE WORDS THAT BEGIN WITH THE LETTER G

Name: _____

DIRECTIONS: WRITE THE WORDS THAT BEGIN WITH THE LETTER H

Name: _____

DIRECTIONS: TRACE THE WORDS THAT BEGIN WITH THE LETTER I

Name: _____

DIRECTIONS: WRITE THE WORDS THAT BEGIN WITH THE LETTER I

Name: _____

DIRECTIONS: WRITE THE WORDS THAT BEGIN WITH THE LETTER J

Name: _____

DIRECTIONS: TRACE THE WORDS THAT BEGIN WITH THE LETTER K

Name: _____

DIRECTIONS: WRITE THE WORDS THAT BEGIN WITH THE LETTER K

Name: _____

DIRECTIONS: TRACE THE WORDS THAT BEGIN WITH THE LETTER L

Name: _____

DIRECTIONS: WRITE THE WORDS THAT BEGIN WITH THE LETTER L

Name: _____

DIRECTIONS: TRACE THE WORDS THAT BEGIN WITH THE LETTER M

Name: _____

DIRECTIONS: WRITE THE WORDS THAT BEGIN WITH THE LETTER M

Name: _____

DIRECTIONS: TRACE THE WORDS THAT BEGIN WITH THE LETTER N

Name: _____

DIRECTIONS: WRITE THE WORDS THAT BEGIN WITH THE LETTER N

Name: _____

DIRECTIONS: TRACE THE WORDS THAT BEGIN WITH THE LETTER O

Name: _____

DIRECTIONS: WRITE THE WORDS THAT BEGIN WITH THE LETTER O

Name: _____

DIRECTIONS: TRACE THE WORDS THAT BEGIN WITH THE LETTER P

Name: _____

DIRECTIONS: WRITE THE WORDS THAT BEGIN WITH THE LETTER P

Name: _____

DIRECTIONS: TRACE THE WORDS THAT BEGIN WITH THE LETTER Q

Name: _____

DIRECTIONS: WRITE THE WORDS THAT BEGIN WITH THE LETTER Q

Name: _____

DIRECTIONS: WRITE THE WORDS THAT BEGIN WITH THE LETTER R

Name: _____

DIRECTIONS: TRACE THE WORDS THAT BEGIN WITH THE LETTER S

Name: _____

DIRECTIONS: WRITE THE WORDS THAT BEGIN WITH THE LETTER S

Name: _____

DIRECTIONS: TRACE THE WORDS THAT BEGIN WITH THE LETTER T

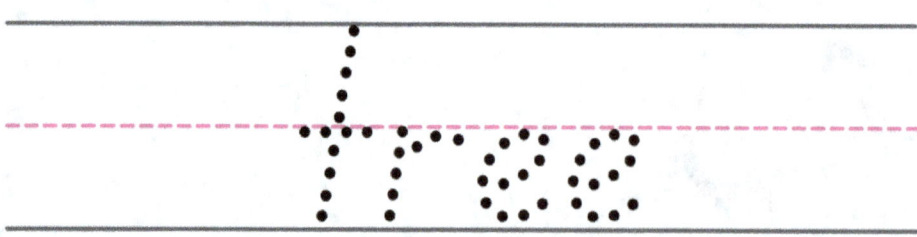
tree

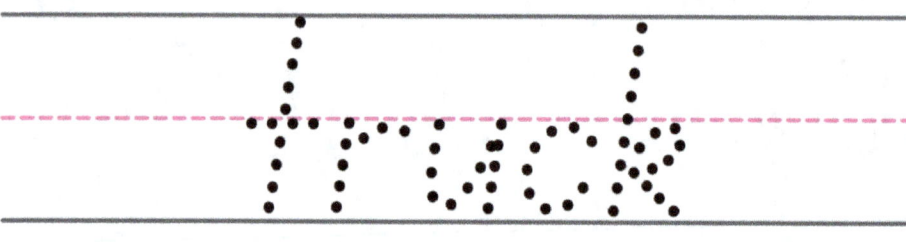
truck

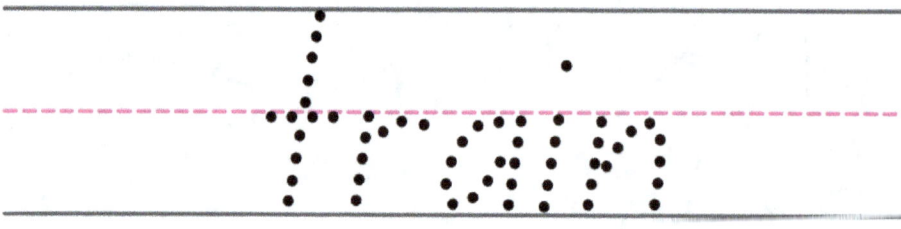
train

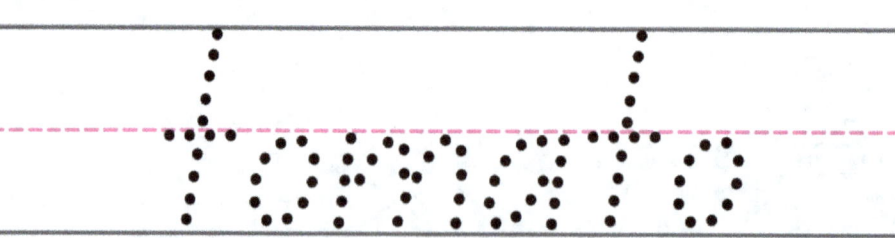
tomato

Name: _____

DIRECTIONS: WRITE THE WORDS THAT BEGIN WITH THE LETTER T

Name: _____

DIRECTIONS: TRACE THE WORDS THAT BEGIN WITH THE LETTER U

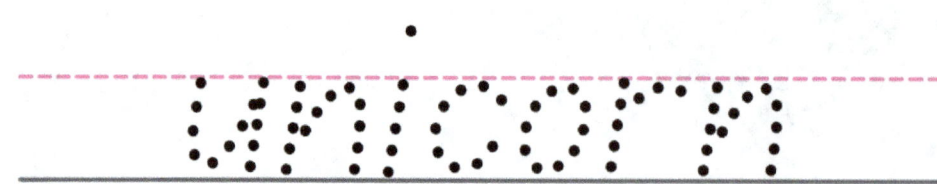
unicorn

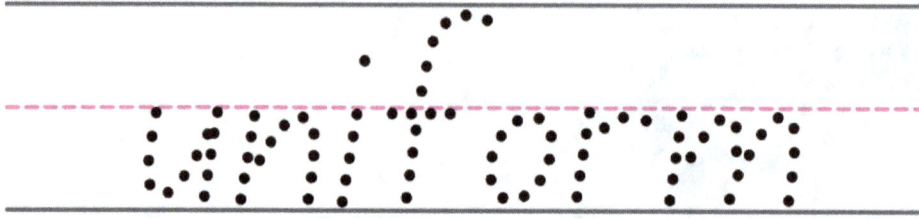
uniform

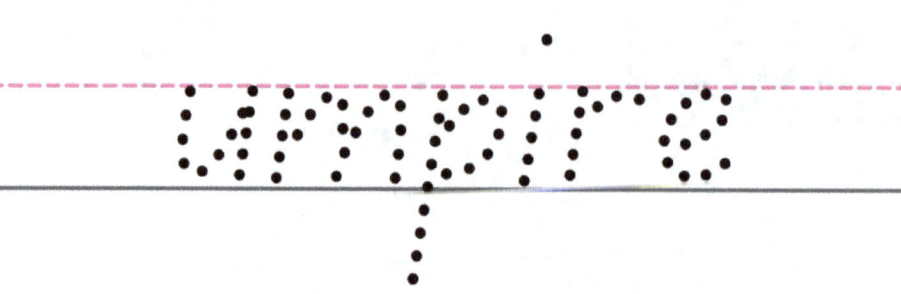
umpire

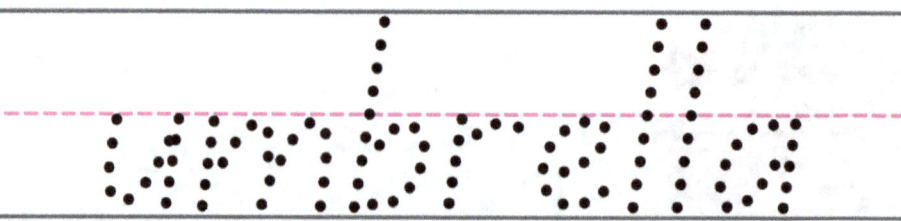
umbrella

Name: _____

DIRECTIONS: WRITE THE WORDS THAT BEGIN WITH THE LETTER U

Name: _____

DIRECTIONS: TRACE THE WORDS THAT BEGIN WITH THE LETTER V

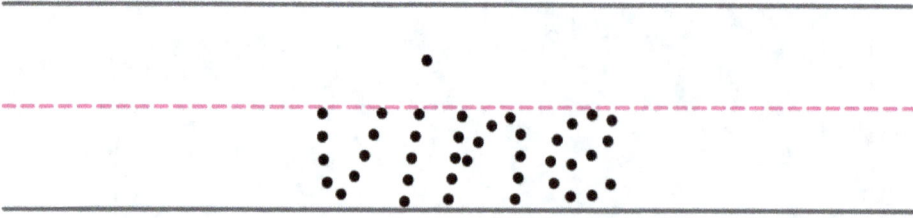
vine

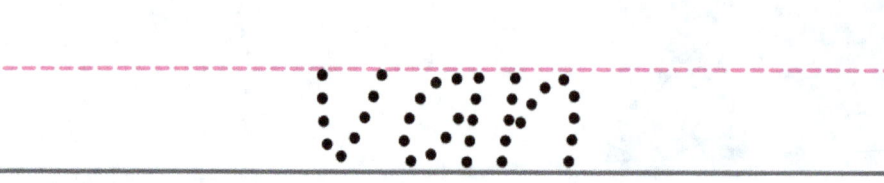
van

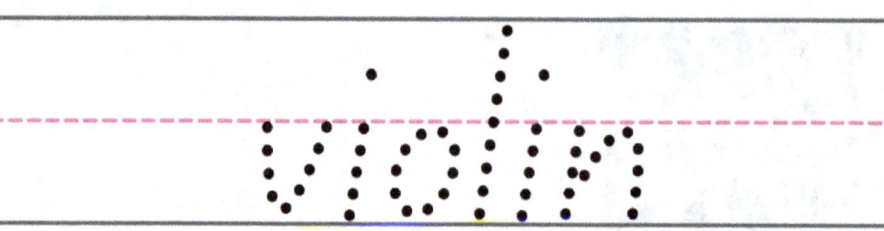
violin

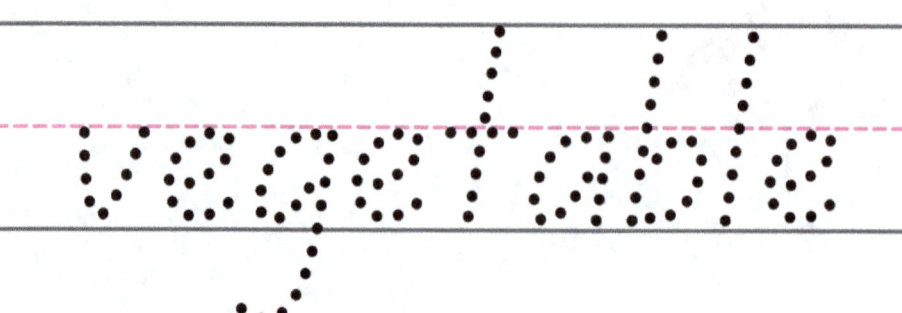
vegetable

Name: _____

DIRECTIONS: WRITE THE WORDS THAT BEGIN WITH THE LETTER V

Name: _____

DIRECTIONS: TRACE THE WORDS THAT BEGIN WITH THE LETTER W

Name: _____

DIRECTIONS: WRITE THE WORDS THAT BEGIN WITH THE LETTER W

Name: _____

DIRECTIONS: TRACE THE WORDS THAT BEGIN WITH THE LETTER X

x-ray

xerox

Xavier

xylophone

Name: _____

DIRECTIONS: WRITE THE WORDS THAT BEGIN WITH THE LETTER X

Name: _____

DIRECTIONS: TRACE THE WORDS THAT BEGIN WITH THE LETTER Y

Name: _____

DIRECTIONS: WRITE THE WORDS THAT BEGIN WITH THE LETTER Y

Name: _____

DIRECTIONS: TRACE THE WORDS THAT BEGIN WITH THE LETTER Z

Name: _____

DIRECTIONS: WRITE THE WORDS THAT BEGIN WITH THE LETTER Z

www.ingramcontent.com/pod-product-compliance
Lightning Source LLC
Chambersburg PA
CBHW051214290426
44109CB00021B/2454